G.

Barrow-in-Furness

in old picture postcards

by
B. Trescatheric
and
J.D. Barker

Third edition

European Library - Zaltbommel/Netherlands MCMLXXXV

GB   ISBN 90 288 2857 5 / CIP

European Library in Zaltbommel/Netherlands publishes among other things the following series:

IN OLD PICTURE POSTCARDS *is a series of books which sets out to show what a particular place looked like and what life was like in Victorian and Edwardian times. A book about virtually every town in the United Kingdom is to be published in this series. By the end of this year about 175 different volumes will have appeared. 1,250 books have already been published devoted to the Netherlands with the title* **In oude ansichten.** *In Germany, Austria and Switzerland 500, 60 and 15 books have been published as* **In alten Ansichten;** *in France by the name* **En cartes postales anciennes** *and in Belgium as* **En cartes postales anciennes** *and/or* **In oude prentkaarten** *150 respectively 400 volumes have been published.*

For further particulars about published or forthcoming books, apply to your bookseller or direct to the publisher.

This edition has been printed and bound by Grafisch Bedrijf De Steigerpoort in Zaltbommel/Netherlands.

INTRODUCTION

The 1882 'Mannex Directory' opened its account of Barrow-in-Furness with the following effusive passage: *The mist of ages does not obscure the origin of Barrow beneath its hazy mantle; nor need we disintombe the musty archives of the Duchy for records of its early history. But yesterday an almost nameless hamlet of some ten or a dozen thatched cottages — today a prosperous corporate town of nearly 50,000 inhabitants, with social conveniences and architectural beauty far surpassing many a town o'er whose head have passed the storms of a thousand years. Barrow is therefore essentially a modern town; and its rise and rapid progress recall to mind those fanciful creations which charmed our youthful days in the pages of the Arabian Nights' Tales. Could some Rip Van Winkle the Second arise from his twenty years' torpor, what would be his surprise, to find perchance the fields where he had basked as the kine lazily browsed in the noonday sun, or the pebbly strand whereon in his boyhood 'he had gathered shells of ocean' now covered with spacious docks, and streets, and houses, and tall chimneys, vomiting forth their dense volumes of black smoke!*

Yet even as this purple prose was being composed, it had become apparent that Barrow's spectacular development was faltering. The next fifty years saw a period of uncertainty, occasionally interrupted by bouts of 'slack times' or much rares flashes of optimism. By the end of the nineteenth century the two architects of Barrow's growth, Schneider and Ramsden, had died and no comparable figures re-placed them. The Furness Railway was in steady decline, hundreds of miners who had moved to Furness in the 1860s and 1870s now left the region as the local mines began to experience severe difficulties. New techniques in smelting and growing foreign competition broke the virtual monopoly which the Barrow and Cumberland Steelworks had once held. As a new century opened the Ironworks closed down for lengthy periods and soup kitchens were set up in Hindpool. Only the arrival of Vickers offered any hope for the future, and their success in winning orders from the Admiralty and foreign navies began to take effect about 1912.

It is true to say that Barrow benefitted from the horrors of the Great War as much as any town in the United Kingdom. An insatiable demand for steel, ships and armaments turned Barrow once more into a 'boom town' with a population of over ninety thousand. But those who confidently predicted that such prosperity would last were to be bitterly disappointed. The half-a-dozen years which followed the ending of the Great War were the most harrowing in Barrow's short history. Thousands were unemployed, almost half the town owed rent and a cruel epidemic of influenza killed literally whole families during the depths of the depression. Recovery was slow and by no means certain when our period ends in 1930.

However, the years 1880 to 1930 offer a paradox, for economic decline was accompanied by definite social progress. A Borough police force was established in 1881, a town library in 1882, and by 1890 the

School Board had created twelve schools offering places to over 7,000 children. The private estate of Vickerstown and the first tentative experiments in municipal housing began to tackle the problem of overcrowding which had afflicted Barrow since the 1860s. With the granting of parliamentary representation in 1885 came political maturity. In local elections the dominant Liberals were opposed by Conservatives, who in turn had to face the challenge of Labour candidates. Some regretted the new political nature of local government, but many more benefitted from its democratisation. A gradual increase in leisure time was reflected in the purchase of Biggar Bank and the development of the Public Park. The 1930 'Barrow Yearbook' lists a multitude of sporting clubs and nine theatres and cinemas. As Barrow slipped further from the dreams of its industrial pioneers it became a better place in which to live, as a third Rip Van Winkle would surely have testified.

Anyone wishing to research Barrow's recent history should consult the following sources: 'Barrow and District' by F. Barnes (a general survey) and 'Furness and the Industrial Revolution' by Dr. J.D. Marshall (a scholarly and stimulating study, invaluable for Barrow 1845-1880). Lancaster University Library holds several theses relevant to Barrow. A mass of information is stored in the Barrow Public Library Local Collection and in the adjoining County Record Office. For photographic material, consult the Library Local Collection and the Furness Museum. This book was commissioned by the publishers to a set format of 116 frames. With such a number it was inevitable that there would be an overlap with previous collections. About a dozen postcards are very similar to views published in Mr. R. Sankey's photo books (1974 and 1978) and a few more have been printed elsewhere. This still leave five-sixths of the photos in our book and many of these will be entirely new to most readers. We have aimed to present the following order: Barrow Views, Industrial, Crowds and Personalities, Walney, Buildings, Ships and Docks, and further Barrow Views. Naturally we have been limited to those postcards and photographs made available to us. An attempt has been made to flesh out the pictures with a text which goes beyond a simple description, but in approximately eighty to one hundred words it is difficult to avoid making generalised statements. The text is the work of B. Trescatheric, who takes full responsibility for the mistakes which will no doubt be eagerly discovered.

Acknowledgements

Most of the postcards and photographs reproduced in this volume were taken from the private collection of Mr. D. Barker. The authors are conscious, however, that without the help of the following people they would not have been able to present as comprehensive a selection: Mr. D.J. Hughes, Curator of the Furness Museum, Dr. W. Rollinson, Senior Lecturer, University of Liverpool, Mr. B. Harrison and Mr. J. Kellett.

1. The classic view of Barrow's Town Hall, ambitious symbol of a grand future which was never realised. Built from Hawcoat sandstone it was designed by Lynn of Belfast, who had won an open competition in 1876. Approval for the building was delayed until 1881; it was finished in 1886, but not officially opened until July 1887 as part of the Victorian Jubilee celebrations. This photograph was taken by H. Bentley, but curiously an identical scene was produced by E. Sankey, which suggests an arranged special session — or shared resources.

2. A horse cab waits patiently in Ramsden Square at the spot which today serves as the Ribble bus terminus. In the background is the Jute Works, but dominating the Square is the statue to Sir James Ramsden – General Manager of the Furness Railway, first Mayor of Barrow and for many years the undisputed 'town boss'. Ramsden was the moving spirit behind several of Barrow's Victorian industries (both successful and unsuccessful) and he inspired the spacious design of the town's major streets. On the debit side he was a domineering individual who attracted respect, but little genuine public admiration.

V350-2 BARROW-IN-FURNESS, RAMSDEN SQUARE, AND DUKE STREET. RAPID PHOTO, E.C

3. A busier scene in Ramsden Square as depicted by a 1909 postcard. The once imposing Square facade included the Cumberland Union Bank and the Lancaster Banking Company, McIntyre and Osborne's Tea House, and a host of professional businesses. At the time of this card they included A.H. Strongitharm (Engineer), Settle and Brundrit (Architects), H. Miller (House and Estate Agent) and several Company offices. The tram carries an advert for a famous Barrow firm, Pass and Co., Wholesale Merchants of Duke Street.

Abbey Road, Barrow-in-Furness

Valentine's Series

4. Horses and steam tram in Abbey Road, from a 1905 postcard. On the right a group leave the new Conservative Club, opened in 1899 by the wife of Barrow's M.P., Sir Charles Cayzer. Sir Charles, the town's first Conservative Member, was to lose his seat in 1906 to Charles Duncan, Barrow's first Labour Representative. Opposite, in more senses than one, is the Working Men's Institute. Opened in 1870 the 'House of Lords' was originally conceived as an improving society for the working men of Barrow, with regular lectures, a library and a games room. As such it inspired a host of similar institutions over the next twenty years.

V350-4   BARROW-IN-FURNESS, ABBEY ROAD   RAPID PHOTO E 6.

5. The view from East Mount looking towards the Town Centre, a 1911 postcard. Abbey Road was planned as a grand avenue into the town which it was once hoped would rival Liverpool. That never happened, but we are left with the legacy of one of the finest entrances to an English provincial town. The East Mount houses were begun in the 1870s as the first suburban development in Barrow. One can trace the infill along Abbey Road as successive blocks of houses were built on the north side. Further from town, grander detached residences accommodated the Victorian elite on the approaches to Furness Abbey.

6. Preston Street in the 1880s, a somewhat euphemistic engraving. It housed an unusual mixture of working men – joiners, plumbers, engineers, bricklayers – and small businesses. Among the latter were Woodburn and Co. (Auctioneers), John Whitley (brush manufacturer) and John Vipond (tailor). On the corner of Preston Street and Dalton Road was the private British School, run by Richard Bailey. Besides being a schoolmaster, he was also a land and insurance agent and had been responsible for organising a group of emigrants to Minnesota in 1873 – as much of a mixture as Preston Street itself!

7. A milk cart trundles past the King's Hall in Hartington Street at the junction with Nelson Street and Drake Street. Opened in 1907, the Hall could seat one thousand, was used chiefly as a Wesleyan meeting place, but could also be hired as public rooms. Both the Primitive and Wesleyan Methodists established chapels in Hartington Street in the 1870s. The earliest houses were solid middle class terraced property; an 1886 Directory lists four surgeons, a dentist (J.W. Carmichael), The Misses Charltons' Ladies School, two builders, three grocers and a solicitor (A.L. Garnett, who was also the Liberal Party agent in Barrow).

DALTON ROAD, BARROW-IN FURNESS

8. Dalton Road, Barrow's main shopping centre, from a postcard sent in 1917. That year a list of shops provides a catalogue of well-remembered businesses – Iliffe (jewellers), Cosimini (confectioners), Mahon (wholesale merchants), Happold (pork butcher), Clay's sixpence bazaar, Schenk (stationer). Other names can still be found – Blair, Brucciani, Davies, Doling, Ward, Rigg, and Melville's Fried Fish Saloon. The 'Bull Hotel', the 'Travellers' Rest' and the 'Bay Horse Inn' no longer survive, but then neither does the 'Watson Temperance Hotel' nor the 'City Temperance Bar'.

Dalton Road, Barrow-in-Furness.

9. Another 1917 card, this time from the Abbey Road end. The Great War brought short-lived prosperity to the town in its role as munitions producer. Wages at the Vickers Works not only increased, for the first time they were being picked up by working girls. A writer sent the following description home: 'The streets at night are one mass of folk, but they will calm down a little after tonight (Sunday) as the girls get back to work tomorrow.' Of the munition girls he said: 'They have been bricks... great fun... they've kept six policemen dash busy round the shell shop.'

10. Furness Park Road in splendid isolation, shortly before the Great War. The photograph was taken opposite what is now the 'Lisdoonie', looking towards Oxford Street. On the left are numbers nine to twenty-nine and on the right is the entrance to Grasmere Road and numbers two to thirty. In the background stands Thorncliffe House; the area between has yet to see the development of the rest of Furness Park Road, Grantley Road and Thornfield Park. The distinctive gables were a feature of Edwardian town architecture.

11. Hawcoat Lane from opposite St. Paul's Church, a 1909 postcard. The rough land in front of Grasmere Road is now the site of a large garage, but was once part of the land covered by Barrow Racecourse. The races were a popular Whitsuntide event in Barrow a hundred years ago and the firm of William Gradwell won the contract to build a grandstand for the Course. He also happened to own the land and his son was on the Race Committee! The houses in the photograph still stand, but the view is now obstructed — what used to be saplings are fully grown trees.

12. A panorama of Barrow Park from a 1924 postcard. Despite regular schemes for a park being put forward in the nineteenth century — one was for an ornamental boating lake on the Steelworks reservoir at Ormsgill — a decision to establish a public park at Risedale was not made until 1900 when £18,000, was borrowed for the purpose. Further delays were caused by difficulty in securing adequate land. It was not until the need to provide relief schemes for the unemployed in the early 1920s that the park was landscaped and the boating lake was built.

9678   NEWBIGGIN BAY.   FURNESS COAST ROAD.   SANKEYS:

13. An identical story lies behind this quiet country scene. The coastal road from Ulverston to Barrow was another relief scheme, built mostly by unemployed Barrow men at a time when the Vickers workforce was only one-eighth of its wartime level. The Coast Road was opened in 1924. This is one of a series of postcards, all featuring the same car — presumably the one used to carry the photographer's gear. On the back of the card the sender enthuses: 'We came back by moonlight on this road. It was lovely.' A modern use for the road has been to divert some of the gas terminal traffic away from the centre of Barrow.

14. This photograph gives some idea of the size of the Hindpool Iron and Steelworks before the process of piecemeal demolition was begun. In the 1870s the Works were the biggest Bessemer steel producers in the World and employed over five thousand men. An estate of terraced housing at Hindpool was laid out to accommodate the migrant labour who flooded into the town, a large proportion coming from the West Midlands. The Iron- and Steelworks' decline began with the Gilchrist – Thomas process which, by allowing the efficient production of steel from phosphoric ore, broke the monopoly of haematite ore. Despite regular bouts of 'slack time' the Ironworks did not close until 1963; a very limited steel operation still survives.

15. Iron mining machinery still in use at Nigel Pit, Roanhead, photographed in the 1920s. The wealth of Barrow was based on the rich haematite mines of Furness — at Lindal, Swarthmoor, Askam, Park, Dalton, Newton, Stank and Roanhead. From approximately 1850 to 1900 they were the props on which rested the Furness Railway and the Hindpool Steelworks. The decline of these industries occurred when the iron ore began to run out or the mines became flooded. The Roanhead pits were owned by the Kennedy family from Ulverston and were one of the last complexes to remain in production. It was not until 1941 that the last commercial shaft was abandoned.

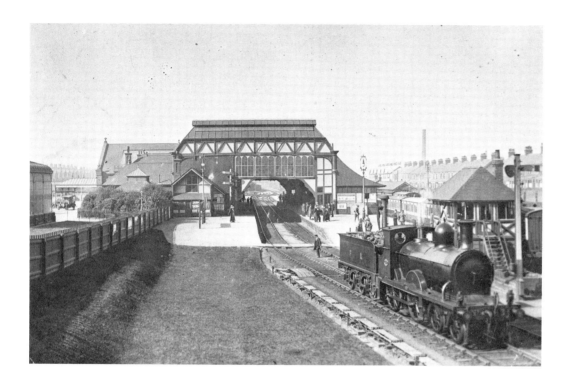

16. A Furness Railway locomotive leaves the Central Station, from a postcard sent in 1916. The writer 'had a nice trip up, but was two hours late as there was a great number of (troops) travelling.' Barrow's first station had been on the Strand at the foot of St. George's Square (part of which is now used as a Railwaymen's Club). The Central Station was opened in 1882 and survived until the night of 7 May 1941, when German bombs demolished most of the buildings. However, the line survived almost intact and trains began running again two days later.

17. Fire damage is evident in this photograph of the Jute Works, on the site now taken up by the John Whinnerah Institute. The Jute Works were opened in 1872, being an attempt to utilise Barrow's new docks and to provide employment for the hundreds of workmen's wives or sweethearts (perhaps wives *and* sweethearts) who were without jobs. Although they became the largest Jute business in England, the Barrow Works could not overcome the near-monopoly of Dundee. Fires in 1879 and 1892 proved to be serious setbacks and the Works closed early this century. The limits of the Works can still be seen, marked today by a white kerbstone in which the stumps of the iron railings are embedded.

18. The towers of the Barrow Saltworks Company, whose works were briefly established at the south end of Walney Island. Extensive salt deposits were discovered in 1891 and a company formed five years later, but competition from the dominant Cheshire saltworks prevented Walney from securing a profitable market share. Closure was followed by intermittent revivals, for example in 1904 and 1909, but the venture was extinct by 1912. It was yet another failure in Barrow's late Victorian attempt to diversify its industrial base. A row of cottages were built at the south end of Walney for Saltworkers and some of these are still in use.

19. Barrow Paperworks at Salthouse, with Cavendish Dock in the background. A Chemical Wood Pulp Company was formed at Barrow in 1888, but in 1892 it was taken over by Kellner-Partington and begin to specialise in paper making. Skilled workers from the Kellner-Partington factory at Glossop were brought to Barrow to boost the new Works and several families settled at Roose village, taking houses left vacant by emigrating iron miners. A new company, Barrow Paper Mills, was formed in 1919 and this remained in business until closure in the 1970s.

'or over 20 years an empty mass of decaying buildings!

20. A postcard issued in the 1920s by Barrow Socialists, complaining of the lack of capital investment in industry at a time of mass unemployment. The Vulcan Works began life as S.J. Claye's Wagon Works, but when he was declared bankrupt in 1881 they were left idle until the Vulcan Steel and Forge Company was formed in 1884. Like another small steel concern — the Griffin Chilled Steel Company off Ainslie Street — the Vulcan Works perpetually struggled, though it was many years before the buildings were finally abandoned. The name is now used for the Council estate built on the site at Salthouse.

21. The Corporation Gas Works at Salthouse, photographed at their opening in February 1917. Barrow Council had taken over the Furness Railway's gasworks on Hindpool Road in 1869 and a steadily rising demand led to the plans for a new purpose-built site at Salthouse. An immediate war-time boost to production was followed by extensions at Salthouse as the old Hindpool plant was phased out. The Works were nationalised in 1949 and eventually closed in 1975 when town gas gave way to natural gas. In the background can be seen Roose Hospital, built a hundred years ago as a model Workhouse.

22. The R80 Airship about to be launched on its flight to Howden. As a later postcard (number 89) depicts, the first airship to be built at Barrow was at the shed on Cavendish Dock. Vickers continued to have faith in the concept and work on the R80 was begun in April, 1918. Suspended for a time at the end of the Great War, it was not completed until 1920. Her maiden trip was a fifteen mile flight over the Irish Sea — modest enough from a ship with a design range of 4,000 miles. On 24 February, 1921 the R80 left Barrow for Howden, and as the card shows she was anchored by a crowd of volunteers until ready for take-off.

23. A few women workers are lost in the expanse of Walney Airship Shed, built at the junction of modern West Shore Road and Cows Tarn Lane. It was to accommodate traffic to the Sheds that Mill Lane was widened into a major thoroughfare. Despite Vickers' commitment the R80 was followed only by one small airship for Japan before the venture was closed down. An attempt was made to sell the Sheds as a cinema studio, but there were no takers for this optimistic idea. Eventually a more prosaic solution was found – the Sheds were sold as scrap to the local firm of J. Brennan and Company.

24. Industry of a different kind depicted in this undated postcard of the Old Cobbler's Shop (old shop or old cobbler?). An 1886 Directory lists one John Lowery as a shoemaker in North Scale, but I do not know if these were his premises. After the Great War the villages of North Scale, Biggar, Hawcoat, Newbarns and Roose became absorbed in the gradual expansion of Barrow. Independent craftsmen were replaced by the services of town centre stores, although as Jack Holgate described in his booklet 'Clatter of Clogs' it was not until the Second World War that the itinerant odd-job man disappeared from Barrow's streets.

3682   SLOOP STREET, BARROW-IN-FURNESS.

25. Washday on Barrow Island, a cliché even in the days before the Great War. Barrow Island was for centuries a peaceful farming island, until in 1871 the Barrow Shipbuilding Company began what was to become a rapid industrial growth. Workers were first housed in the infamous Barrow Island Huts – sordid rows of wooden barracks without any sanitary services. The Devonshire Buildings were built in two phases in the 1870s and 1880s and were based on the high-density Scotch model flats. Their continued existence is proof of general soundness, but even when they were built alternative forms of advanced terraced housing were available elsewhere. The oppressive monotony of the flats served only to reinforce the discipline of the work regime.

26. A mass of Vickers Workers on the High Level Bridge, a postcard sent in 1912. The writer commented: 'Some stock, eh? They'd fill Highgate. They do cover the High Level Bridge anyway. The World's workers, backbone of the Empire.' You can see from the front three rows that the Empire's back had some very young bones. Vickers employed about 14,000 men in 1912, having risen during the period of pre-war expansion from some 9,000 in 1909. Although the Vickers Works were popularly known as the Shipyard, then – as now – the majority of workers were employed on the engineering side.

27. A proud assembly by the Salvation Army Band, although I am not certain where the photograph was taken. The Salvation Army was founded at Barrow in January 1881 and seems to have been afforded a generally tolerant welcome. A rally was held in March 1882 to celebrate '14 months of zealous activity', during which time £160 had been sent to General Booth for Army uses. The 'earnestness and sincerity' of the first 'Hallelujah Lasses' overcame any irreverence and Barrow did not witness the 'brutal opposition, fierce persecution and vulgar row' of such places as Sheffield, Bolton and Oldham.

28. A busy scene at the Town Market, Barrow's first 'superstore'! The original indoor market was ninety feet by forty-five feet and built by James Garden for the Furness Railway in 1866. It formed part of a civic complex which included the Old Public Hall, Police Station and Municipal Offices in Lawson Street. It was taken over by the new Barrow Corporation in 1867 and expansion saw the addition of a glass roof over half an acre of adjoining space. Barrow market attracted a host of local tradesmen and characters – 'Fish Maggie', the 'Celery King' – and survived in this form until the late 1960s.

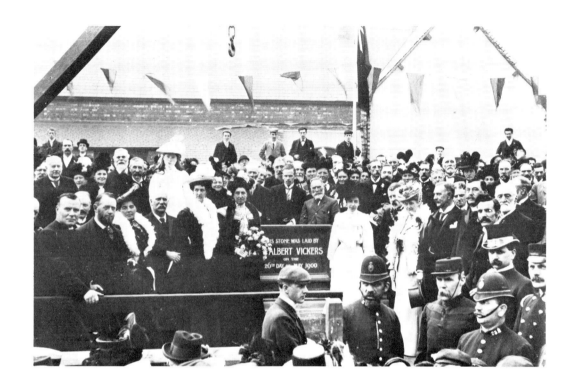

29. Mrs. Albert Vickers laying the foundation stone of the Technical School in Abbey Road, 26 May 1900. The new school was designed as a further education centre for artisans in the town's principal industries and Mr. Vickers spoke at the ceremony of the 'need to promote science and efficiency in industry at a time of increasing foreign competition'. Enclosed in the foundation stone was a sealed bottle containing coins, a list of Councillors, copies of the local daily paper, and a directory of the Barrow School of Business and Art for the session 1899-1900.

WAITING FOR THE FERRY

30. Shipyard workers wait for the Walney Ferry, photographed some two years before the opening of the Bridge. No wonder the Furness Railway welcomed the building of Vickerstown. It turned a ferry loss of £800 per annum into a profit of £1,000 per annum. Such was the traffic that the landing stage cobbles were worn flat by hobnailed boots. However, the sender of the card had more festive thoughts than ferries and work: 'Tattie is very busy making Christmas plum puddings and she wants me to stay and help her.'

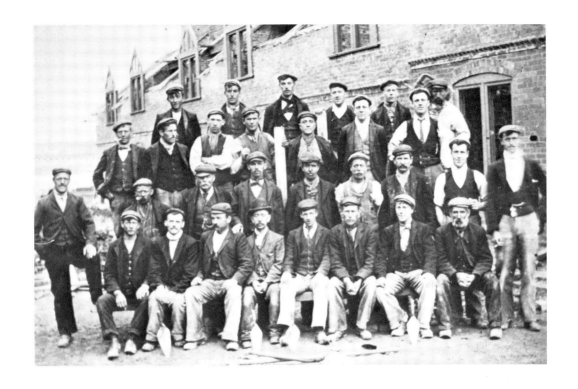

31. A group of building site workers on Vickerstown, with trowels stuck ceremoniously in the ground. Vickerstown was built by several firms, some of them outsiders, but including local contractors such as Gradwell and Co., Walton Lee and Co., Rainey Brothers, James Cox, and Robinson and Clark. The original accommodation for site workers was a novel reconstruction of an iron methodist chapel formerly in Brighton Street, re-erected on Walney in 1899. A second, more orthodox, hut was built the following year.

32. A parade in the vicinity of Paxton Terrace to celebrate Barrow hosting the national Church Congress in 1906. A week's events began on 29 September and included Church meetings, services and public lectures. Two of these were entitled Church and Parental Responsibility (Training – Hygiene, Temperance, Purity) and The Church and The People (Socialism and the Unemployed in Christian England). Throughout the week there was an Ecclesiastical Art Exhibition in the Drill Hall on the Strand.

BARROW HOSPITAL PARADE. SEPT. 19TH, 1908.

33. A section of the 1908 Hospital Parade passes through Church Street. Among the bands taking part were the Cumberland and Westmorland Imperial Yeomanry Band, the Vickers Shipyard Band and the Millom Wesleyan Temperance Band. Several departments in Vickers and the Steelworks provided decorated floats and dancing troupes filled the streets. Thousands of people attended the afternoon gala at Cavendish Park and the proceedings were finished with an evening torchlight parade led by the Salvation Army Band and, appropriately, the Fire Brigade. Over £500 was raised to improve and extend the hospital buildings.

34. A photograph taken just before the launch of a Japanese warship. Three vessels were built at Barrow for the Imperial Japanese Navy – the 'Mikasa', the 'Katori' and the 'Kongo'. All were launched with the traditional accompaniment of a balloon of doves, which were released once the ship entered the water. The crew of the 'Mikasa' became well known in Barrow as they spent a few months in the town as the ship was being fitted-out. They had their own social club and were lodged in the cabins of the old liner, 'Alaska', which Vickers had previously used as emergency accommodation for its workers.

35. On board the 'Lady Evelyn' as it pulls out of Barrow Docks. Between 1901 and 1913 the Furness Railway provided a summer boat service between Barrow and Fleetwood, mainly for Blackpool holiday makers visiting the Lakes. The duties were shared by the 'Lady Evelyn', 'Lady Moyra', 'Lady Margaret' and 'Philomel', although at peak times the tug 'Walney' was also pressed into service. The trips were never resumed following the disruption caused by the Great War. 'Lady Moyra' and 'Lady Evelyn' were sold and became the 'Brighton Queen' and 'Brighton Belle'. Both were lost during the Dunkirk evacuation.

36. A fine example of the street decorations which appeared in Hindpool during the Coronation celebrations of Edward VII in August 1902. On the afternoon of 9 August there were public sports in the Park and a regatta on Walney Channel. In the evening a torchlight procession congregated to sing the National Anthem outside the Town Hall, which had been especially illuminated by gas jets. The best private street decorations were to be seen in Hindpool and there was a particularly keen rivalry between the occupants of Hood and Howe Streets.

37. From a public ceremony to a private occasion. This family portrait is typical of thousands which came out of Barrow's Victorian photo studios, often taken to mark a birth or a wedding anniversary, but also to keep in touch with relations during a period of frequent labour migration. Shirkcliffe Priest was one of four photographers listed in Roberts' 1886 Directory — Frank Fell (Duke Street), Davis and Sons (Abbey Road) and Charles Richards (Duke Street) were the others. Priest retained his Paxton Terrace studio until the Great War, after which it was taken over by another photographer, H. Bentley.

38. Ready for the off are the Walker Brothers and Teddie Trelfor, photographed in 1888 at the old Parade Ground (this side it now covered by the Fire Station and Dental Laboratories). Barrow Amateur Cycle Club were holding championships as early as 1876 and the penny-farthings, now regarded as museum pieces, were then the speediest and most manouverable machines available. The Walkers – from the left, James, William and Tom – were famous sportsmen of their day. In 1878 William won a gold medal for a half-mile race in Barrow Baths, plus a prize for 'ornamental swimming'.

39. A languid pose from members of the Cavendish (Rugby) Football Club. Rugby was quickly established at Barrow and the town team was formed in 1875. A host of local sides included St. George's, Union Jack, Roose, Ulverston Grasshoppers and Askam. The number of players could range from ten to twenty-five and rules were often agreed at the start of the match by each side's umpire. By the 1880s, however, the sport was becoming regulated and the Barrow Club ventured across the Pennines on several Yorkshire tours. Organised sport was still a mainly middle-class pursuit, but the mining teams of Roose and Askam gave a new meaning to 'class struggle'.

40. A fearsome set of opponents for anyone – the 1916 Munition Girls' football team in full battle dress. During the Great War about six thousand munition workers were employed at Barrow and this demand was only fully met by bringing in girls from the Lancashire mill towns. Hostels were built at Chapel Lane, Walney, the Old Baths on Abbey Road and Victoria Hall in Rawlinson Street. The soccer team was one of the many attempts made to put the girls' spare time to healthy and wholesome use. At the close of the War all the 'mob caps' were quickly paid off. None ever managed to play for Bolton Wanderers.

41. A fighting pose from Butcher Moore, one of Barrow's most famous boxers from a period when two or three promotions were held every month. Butcher fought for almost thirty years and was the star of many a comeback. As a young docker at Douglas, Isle of Man, he once worked a morning shift in order to run a fifteen mile race in the afternoon; that night he boxed a twelve round draw and on his way home he rescued a dock policemen who had been blown off a jetty into the sea. For this act of bravery he received a vellum testimonial and inscribed medal from Lord Raglan.

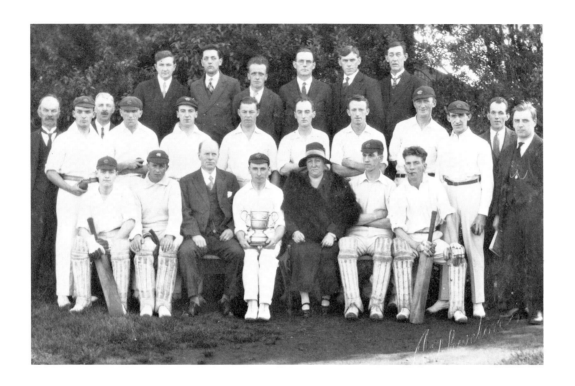

42. Roose Cricket Club, team and committee members, in the late 1920s. A cricket team was formed at Roose soon after the creation of the modern village in the early 1870s. It was a community of mostly Cornish iron miners and its cricket and rugby sides were purely of local composition – full of Harveys, Pascoes, Richards, Trelores. When this postcard was produced the team was still a village affair, often accompanied to away fixtures by a bus load of supporters. The same was true of other local teams – Askam, Lindal, Dalton. Times change, though some will say that the colour of Roose pads does not.

43. A noble pose struck by William Gradwell, master
builder and Mayor of Barrow 1881-1882. He built up
his business from a small carpentry yard at Roose to a
point where he employed hundreds of men as builders,
joiners and brickmakers. Some of the current town
buildings he constructed are the Working Men's
Institute, Holker Street School, the Amphitheatre
(Palace) and his firm was responsible for hundreds of
houses on the Hindpool estate. As a Councillor he was
a solid supporter of the Railway — Steelworks
Establishment. He was Barrow's fifth Mayor, but
tragically died in office on 6 September 1882 at Shap
Wells, where 'he had gone for the sake of his health'.

44. Corporal McDowell receives his award for bravery from Sir Alfred Barrow, 16 February 1917. William McDowell of Vengeance Street was awarded the Military Medal at his old Vickerstown School just over three months after going out under enemy shelling at Le Fermont to repair telephone communication wires. In the background, with the dark moustache, is 'Boss' Thompson, the first Headmaster of Vickerstown School and formerly of Roose School. The ceremony unfortunately had a sad ending, for Mr. McDowell was to suffer considerably from the effects of gas poisoning received at the Front.

45. A relaxed study of a youthful Bram Longstaffe, socialist campaigner and Mayor of Barrow 1934-1936. Longstaffe was a committed left-winger and supporter of the Russion Revolution. During the Great War he was imprisoned as a Conscientious Objector but his stand was perhaps vindicated by his election as Councillor for Walney in 1919. Although he became an Alderman and Mayor, Bram Longstaffe never lost his early zeal and abrasiveness. He devoted much of his political career to the education of young Labour Party members, and his sudden death on 16 October 1942 came as a great shock to thousands of Barrovians.

46. The long awaited bridge to Walney under construction, in 1906. The bridge was built to replace Walney Ferry and followed a fierce campaign by the residents of the new township of Vickerstown. Previous schemes had failed to prove a need for a Walney bridge but the hundreds of workmen who travelled from Walney to Vickers provided an unanswerable case. A public poll in 1904 voted two to one for the bridge and work began the following year. It was a toll bridge until 1935 when it was freed as part of the Jubilee celebrations.

47. A packed tram glides across Walney Bridge. The tram service was opened in June 1909 as far as the Promenade and two years later the extension to Biggar Bank was completed. This was mainly a tourist line and the trams terminated at Amphitrite Street during the winter months. A Corporation advert in 1921 promoted Biggar Bank as an ideal Whitsuntide holiday outing: 'You will have the same sea, sky and air as Blackpool, at less expense'. A tram shelter is still in place on Walney Promenade at the foot of Central Drive.

WALNEY BRIDGE, BARROW·IN·FURNESS. (17)   221151. J.V.

48. Ferry Beach on Barrow Island at a time when it was a popular bathing spot. Despite its peaceful setting, Walney Channel claimed several lives in the last century, especially when revellers missed the last Ferry and tried to swim home. One private ferryman, Anthony Strong, rescued more than a dozen people in difficulties. Strong had been a champion oarsman in the 1870s when races attracted large prizes and considerable gambling. In the background is Walney Theatre, opened in November 1915 as a private venture, replacing a proposed community Vickerstown Picture Palace in Mill Lane.

49. A close-up view of the second Walney Ferry. When dredging operations destroyed the ancient fords to Walney, the Furness Railway (responsible for the docks and channel) began a Ferry service, which was to meet Walney's needs until the building of Vickerstown. Then the Ferry, 'old Wana's friend', became 'modern Vickerstown's torturer'. Vickers ran a rival Ferry, nicknamed the 'Mudlark', from the Works to the steps at Empress Drive. When the bridge was opened the Ferry was withdrawn from service, used in Barrow Docks for a while and then sold to Southampton for use as a travelling bridge across the River Test.

Barrow-in-Furness.

James Dunn Park and Shipyard.

The Wrench Series, No. 4684

50. The James Dunn Park, now called Vickerstown Park, in its Edwardian heyday. Named after the Naval Director at Vickers Yard, the Park was opened in 1902 although it was another two years before all the attractions were installed. These included a bandstand, concert stage, refreshment kiosks and a swan pond, from which the swans were liable to escape into the channel. A nursery produced flowers and vegetables for sale to Vickerstown tenants. The park was transferred to the care of the Barrow Corporation in the winter of 1914-1915, at about which time Central Drive was constructed along its southern boundary.

WALNEY.

ROYAL PIERROTS.

51. Entertaining the crowd in James Dunn Park about 1905, with the Ferry waiting in the background. Pierrots were a popular late Victorian and Edwardian concert party, derived from characters in traditional French pantomime and combining songs, juggling and athletic buffoonery. They were one of the attractions which could bring as many as seven thousand visitors to the Park on a bank holiday. Regular concerts were given from the bandstand by the Shipyard Band, the Walney Male Voice Choir or even the shortlived Vickerstown Orchestra.

3424   PROMENADE & DOUGLAS STREET, VICKERSTOWN, WALNEY ISLAND.   SANKEY.

52. A postcard sent in 1924 after the development of Vickerstown. Two workers' estates were built from 1899 to 1906 – North and South Vickerstown – and about 950 houses were finished in this period. They were built to fit the concept of a model industrial village, but a grander claim that Vickerstown was a 'marine garden city' could not be justified. A second phase of building, of a more subdued design, took place just before and during the Great War. Building the estates was the only way in which Vickers could house the skilled workers they needed to attract from Clydeside and the North-East.

MIKASA STREET WALNEY

53. Playtime at the junction of Mikasa Street and Ocean Road. The Mikasa houses were built for skilled craftsmen and foremen and rented at seven shillings per week. Included in the rent was a charge for repairs and decoration, carried out by the Estate Company's workforce. This resulted in the houses having a uniform appearance, long since gone from multi-coloured Vickerstown. The children are aptly congregating on the site of what was to become the Ocean Road School. A temporary structure was built in 1905 but it was 1917 before the permanent School was opened.

54. 'HMS Powerful' being guided through Walney Channel after her launch on 24 July 1895. When the Navel Construction Company took over from the Barrow Shipbuilding Company in 1888 it inherited a workforce of 872 men. Specialisation in Government contracts, mostly warships, meant that when the yard was bought by Vickers in 1897 the number of employees had risen to five and a half thousand. The 'Powerful' was used in a variety of naval roles until it was declared obsolete and became an accommodation ship in the Great War. Renamed 'Impregnable II' in 1919 it was eventually broken up at Blyth in 1929...

POWERFUL ST VICKERSTOWN.

55. It also gave its name to this street in Vickerstown, along with other ships such as 'Hogue', 'Dominion', 'Juno', 'Doris' and 'Niobe'. Powerful Street was finished in 1904, being larger houses rented for eight shillings per week. In the 1950s they were offered for sale to sitting tenants for prices ranging from £400 to £500. The electric light was a proud possession, installed firstly on North Vickerstown – the South estate had to tolerate oil lamps for another year or two, one of the many causes of a North versus South rivalry in the early days of Vickerstown: echoes of which could be heard for many years.

56. Another bridge on Walney, but this time one built to take bricks from the south brickworks (now the site of Liverpool Street) to the northern estate. In the background the houses of what became French Street are partly finished. Other streets on the northern estate were also named after Boer War generals — White, Roberts, Kitchener, Baden Powell — giving a curious mix of naval and army sounds. The Vickerstown Bridge was in use until the North Scale brickworks came into full production in 1902. Many older Vickerstown residents still remember the James Dunn Park as being called 'Bridge Valley'.

57. Pastoral Walney contrasted with the industry of Hindpool across the Channel. James Dunn Park had yet to be laid out and the hill behind the Ferry was still a natural sandpit. The Ferry Hotel was at the time owned by Ind. Coope and Company, but it later became one of a chain of public houses – the King Alfred, the George – owned by the Vickerstown Public Trust. This was a community association which encouraged pubs to sell non-alcoholic refreshment and used part of the profits to fund civic societies. In the 1920s the Ferry Hotel was sold to James Thompson and Company.

58. This can hardly be a launch crowd for they are looking the wrong way. Perhaps it was taken during one of the Vickerstown Regattas held regularly before the Great War. In the background is the Ferry Hotel with the Estate Company's office alongside and next to Chairmans Walk. For many years the Promenade was left unfinished until the Rainey Brothers secured a contract to tarmacadam the surface. No sooner had this been done than it had to be dug up to lay a new gas supply to the island. Such things were not supposed to happen in the old days!

Parish Church, Walney, Barrow.

59. The bell tower being inspected at St. Mary's Church some time before the latest alterations. A Church has been in existence at Walney for a little over four hundred years, the vicar having been supported by tithes from Walney farmers and the rent from Church land. At least two rebuildings of the Church were recorded before the influx of population into Vickerstown once again made expansion necessary. An ornate design was drawn up in 1906, but this had to be abandoned in favour of a cheaper conversion, carried out in fits and starts from 1908 until 1930.

PROCESSION TO NEW CHURCH WALNEY
OCT. 3ᴿᴰ 1908.

60. Part of the celebration parade held to commemorate the beginning of the Church rebuilding. These children from the Sunday School had assembled at the Parish Hall in Knox Street, built in 1902 by Gradwell and Company, but paid for by Vickers in return for the sale of Church land needed to widen the Promenade. The building of Vickerstown also led to the founding of a Methodist Church on the Promenade and a Presbyterian Church in Albert Street (see postcard 52) — the latter to serve the strong Scottish presence on the island.

61. Biggar Village in 1900, with the fore-runner of modern Carr Lane on the right. Biggar is a derivative from the Norse 'byggergh', perhaps meaning a barley pasture. The old name for Walney was Hougenai or the island of Hougun, the latter being the name of the Low Furness peninsula recorded in the Domesday Book. In the centre of the photograph stands Biggar Dyke, a medieval defence against sea flooding, built and maintained by the villagers. Supervision of the dyke was one of the duties of Biggar's grave (Mayor) and painlooker (treasurer). Although overgrown and neglected, the dyke still stands and is best seen from the channel side.

62. The crumbling walls of Trough Head Cottage, on the western coast of Walney, soon to be swept away by sea erosion when photographed in 1900. The farmstead was mapped as being some hundred and twenty yards from the shoreline in the eighteenth century but by the 1840s this had been reduced to forty yards and the last traces vanished in 1902. It has been estimated that the site now lies thirty yards out to sea, a graphic illustration of the process by which material is being carried away from Walney's western shore and being deposited on the northern and southern tips of the island.

A 472-32   OLD WINDMILL AND NORTH SCALE FARM, WALNEY ISLAND.

63. Another photograph of decay, but this time the result of the march of technological change. Windmills on Walney date back to the 1550s, the first being on the western coast at the point where modern Mill Lane begins. This mill ended its life in the early eighteenth century; the North Scale Mill was built during a 'corn boom' in the 1800s — certainly by 1813 — and continued in use for about sixty years. It was not finally demolished until 1940 during the creation of Walney Aerodrome.

Biggar Bank. Walney Island.

RELIABLE WH SERIES.

64. An early postcard of Biggar Bank and its Pavilion. The Bank was purchased by Barrow Corporation in 1881 after a five year campaign to claim it as open land. Tenant farmers had tried to erect fences, only for organised groups of steelworkers – the 'Hindpool Lambs' – to be ferried to Walney to pull them down. On the official opening of the Bank on Good Friday 1883 it was described as 'where the Barrovian loved to smoke the pipe of peace', but there would have been precious little peace on that day as an estimated twenty thousand visitors sampled the fresh sea breezes. The Pavilion survived until January 1976.

65. There was once a fashion for dressing-up at the seaside rather than stripping off. Nevertheless the sender of this card had braved the elements: 'Fine weather. We are by the sea, the tide was grand this morning.' When Vickerstown was originally planned there was a short-lived scheme to create a holiday resort on the west coast, to be called Walney-on-Sea. A newspaper account forecast 'huge hotels, lines of cooking houses, big wheels, palmists, penny-a-ride donkeys', but then the reporter pinched himself and 'it was all a vision and whether I am the only dreamer, time will show'.

WEST SHORE, WALNEY ISLAND, BARROW-IN-FURNESS.

66. A holiday scene at West Shore in the 1920s, viewed from what is now the Roundhouse, looking towards Sandy Gap. A Great War tank serves as a memorial, and a reminder that Biggar Bank was taken over by the Military during that campaign. After the War the Corporation claimed hundreds of pounds in compensation for damage caused by enthusiastic trench digging. There is an interesting mix of transport at the corner – horse and cart, bicycle, and an early motorbike. This area was later the site for Walney Open Air Baths, built as an unemployment relief project in 1931.

A 120/35 BIGGAR BANK, WALNEY ISLAND. THE PUTTING GREEN. SANKEYS.

67. Trying to read the green on the 'Eighteenth', with Brucciani's ice-cream parlour forming a modest clubhouse. Many attempts were made to promote Biggar Bank and West Shore into more than just a local weekend playground. There was a scheme for an elaborate Brine Baths and luxury hotel in 1901, a miniature golf course, and a fun fair. In the 1940s the Corporation had plans for a comprehensive site including holiday camp, ornamental gardens, marine park and hotels. Lack of capital and the chronic problem of isolation prevented any such development.

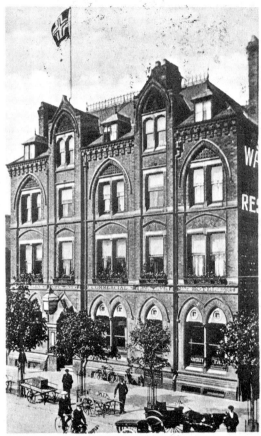

WAVERLEY HOTEL, BARROW-IN-FURNESS
Telephone 590   Mrs. J. B. SANSOM, Proprietress
Telegrams: "Waverley, Barrow"

68. A promotional postcard of the Waverley Hotel on Abbey Road — the flag looks as if it has been painted in. The Waverley was a temperance 'family and commercial' hotel, opened in the 1880s, and surviving until the night of 16 April 1941. A Warden's log details: '00.57 fire at back of Baths, 01.18 ambulance required at Waverley Hotel, 01.20 messenger reports great damage to Plaza, Baths, Ritz'. On the Baptist Church roof the Minister and a helper were killed on firewatch duty. The site of the Church and Waverley is now occupied by the Coronation Gardens.

BAPTIST CHURCH, *BARROW-IN-FURNESS*

Davis Photo.

69. The Baptist Church on Abbey Road which was destroyed in the 1941 Blitz. When the great waves of immigrant workers flooded into Barrow in the middle of the nineteenth century, they brought with them their nonconformist religious beliefs. In 1853 the first Baptist 'chapel' was a sod hut near South End Farm on Walney. Meetings were later held in private houses and the Preston Street Schoolroom (above H. Samuel the Jewellers), until the Abbey Road Church was opened in 1873. A similar story could be told of the early days of Barrow's Methodists, Congregationalists and Presbyterians.

70. St. John's Church on Barrow Island, one of four churches consecrated on the same day, 26 September 1878 – St. Luke's, St. Matthew's, St. Mark's and St. John's. The need for a church on Barrow Island was evident once the Barrow Iron Shipbuilding Company founded its yard there in 1870. A collection of temporary barracks and later blocks of flats were built to house a rapidly expanding population. The original St. John's Church was made of wood and brick but was replaced in 1935 by a concrete structure, with a distinctive outline. Alongside on the photograph is the first St. John's School.

71. The original St. Paul's Church at the corner of Abbey Road and Hawcoat Lane. The first established church in Newbarns was a 'chapel of ease' on land at Far Stackwood, Risedale (now occupied by 251 Abbey Road). A school was built and used for services until St. Paul's was erected in 1871, with Thomas Goss as the first vicar. In 1878 a new school was opened in Hawcoat Lane. St. Paul's has seen much modernisation work in the twentieth century, some of it being necessary to repair slight bomb damage during the Second World War.

72. 'The Riddle Rider' setting a daily puzzle at the Electric Theatre in the 1920s. The Electric was opened in 1910 and was Barrow's first purpose-built cinema. In its first year the other places of amusement were the Royalty Theatre and Opera House in Cavendish Street, His Majesty's Theatre in Albert Street, the Tivoli in Forshaw Street and the New Hippodrome at Rawlinson Street. The Electric was nick-named 'Laugh and Scratch', having an undeserved reputation as a flea pit. In fact it had a regular clientele who rarely visited other cinemas. Such loyalty was reflected in the continued use of piano accompaniment long after it had disappeared elsewhere.

Station Barrow

73. The Furness Railway headquarters in St. George's Square, an historic landmark which was tragically allowed to decay and then demolished a few years ago. When Furness Railway chose Barrow village as its headquarters in 1846 it signalled the beginning of the modern town and eventually stimulated the development of Ironworks, Engineering Works and shipbuilding. The Railway owned most of the land on which Barrow was built and for many years the Board meetings in the St. George's offices effectively made decisions on behalf of the town. Even when Barrow became a Borough with its own Council in 1867, the earliest civic meetings continued to be held at the Railway headquarters.

A 383   INFIELD CONVALESCENT HOME.   SAWKEYS.

74. Infield House in the days when it stood in its own grounds off Abbey Road. The mansion was built in the 1870s for S.J. Claye, the proprietor of Salthouse Wagon Works. When Claye went bankrupt in 1882 the house was empty for two years until purchased by the Barrow builder, Benjamin Fish. In 1892 it was sold to T.F. Butler (Mayor of Barrow 1906-1911) and after the Great War it became the property of Vickers. For many years it was used as a War Memorial Convalescent Home, but was finally demolished in April 1968. The name is retained by the houses which form Infield Gardens, Crescent and Park.

75. Barrow Cenotaph, a postcard issued soon after it had been unveiled on Armistice Day 1921. It was presented to the town by the Barrow Haematite Steel Company, designed by Major Oakley of Barrow and sculpted by a local firm, Fairbairn and Hull. In February 1924 a scheme to illuminate the memorial at night was begun, with electric light being supplied by Barrow Corporation free of charge. The dramatic silhouette could be seen clearly from Dalton and Melton Hill. The Cenotaph stands in the Park on what was called Black Hill, thought to be a prehistoric defensive site, and if so a strangely fitting location.

A89   COLISEUM BUILDINGS, ABBEY ROAD, BARROW-IN-FURNESS.   SANKEY.

76. A full frontal shot of the Coliseum, used as a cinema and for live theatre, including a 1948 production of 'The Nude Look', 'the revue banned by the Purity League'. The 'Colly' was built in 1914 on the site of Zelva's Hippodrome and by the 1920s – when it was owned by C. and M. Routledge Ltd. – was one of eight cinemas and theatres in the town. A local cinema expert has written that in 1929 the Coliseum showed the first talkie in Barrow, but that honour has always been a matter of fierce debate among old film fans. The Coliseum was closed for several years before being demolished in 1977.

A83   RAMSDEN SQUARE AND FREE PUBLIC LIBRARY, BARROW-IN-FURNESS.   SANKEYS.

77. Barrow Public Library, which Pevsner, the noted architectural critic, describes as being 'Beaux-Arts Classical, well handled'. The town's first civic library was housed in a temporary iron building at Schneider Square from 1882 until 1887, when it was incorporated into the new Town Hall. In 1922 the purpose-built Ramsden Square library was opened, after having been postponed during the Great War because of labour shortage. A museum was created on the upper floor in 1930. Branch libraries were established at Walney, Salthouse and Barrow Island in the 1940s. The library was transferred to Cumbria County Council in 1974.

Barrow-in-Furness.   The Schools. Vickerstown.

The Wrench Series, No. 4681

78. Vickerstown School in Latona Street, elegantly poised behind the septic tank which served North
Vickerstown. The school was officially opened in August 1902, its ten classrooms and central hall
being designed to accommodate 648 children. Two years later it had 754 on the attendance roll and
prefabricated iron classrooms had to be added. In the early months of the Great War the Latona Street
school was taken over by the military for the emergency billeting of troops. Children were scattered to
the Methodist Church Hall, the Public Hall and even a giant marquée rented from the Furness Railway.

79. A country scene depicting Little Mill, the building which gave its name to Mill Brow near Furness Abbey. It was once one of three water mills which were powered by a two mile stretch of Abbey Beck — Roose Mill (near the footbridge opposite Roose Station) and Abbey Mill were the others. In the 1870s the Furness Railway bought Little Mill and Roose Mill and used them for many years as accommodation for staff. The site of the now-demolished mill can still be traced by the footpath which leads from the Abbey to Dalton. And the beck? Its course was changed to facilitate a Railway branch line.

80. The rural splendour of Abbotswood Mansion in its own grounds near Furness Abbey. In 1857 the Furness Railway agreed to build a residence for James Ramsden, Railway Superintendent and later Manager. It was completed within a few years, mainly of Hawcoat sandstone, and Ramsden lived there until his death in 1896. Abbotswood was rented accommodation throughout Sir James' tenancy, but his son Frederick Ramsden was able to secure the lease. Eventually, in the 1950s, it became the property of the War Department. In 1961 Barrow Corporation took it over as a civil defence base, but the cost of upkeep was such that it was demolished a few years later.

81. Waiting for the Three O'Clock at Furness Abbey's picturesque station, a postcard produced for the Furness Railway by Raphael Tuck and Sons. This station served the needs of the Abbey Hotel and was also the stop for visitors to the Abbey itself. But perhaps its most famous customer was Sir James Ramsden. The satirical magazine, 'Barrow Vulcan', regularly carried complaints of long delays on the Railway while the train waited for Sir James to embark from Abbotswood. Was this the first example of flexible rostering?

82. Afternoon tea on the lawn with the Furness Abbey Hotel providing an imposing background. The former Manor House was bought by the Furness Railway as a tourist hotel and a base for Railway guests as early as 1847. Even by that date there were plans to run a steamer service from Piel to Fleetwood, but it was some fifty years later that the Hotel became an integral part of the Railway's tourist programme. In 1900 it was advertised as being the ideal centre from which to sample the Lake tours or a trip to the Isle of Man. The hotel was demolished soon after the Second World War, but part of it remains in use as a restaurant.

83. On the verandah at the Abbey Hotel in its Edwardian prime. The scene is a cross between an elegant conservatory of a Country House and a First Class railway waiting room. Tourist posters and a Furness Railway timetable adorn the wall. Inside, the Hotel contained stained glass and stone and marble carvings from the Abbey, the latter now being part of the Furness Museum's collection. As late as the 1930s the Hotel had a staff of over forty maids, porters, cooks and clerks.

Furness Abbey and Hotel

Stengel & Co., London E. C. 39 Redcross Street 17094

84. A late Victorian card showing Furness Abbey before it was carefully trimmed and ordered. The Abbey was founded in 1127 and prospered until its dissolution four hundred years later. Its size was a testimony to the wealth of the Abbey — derived mainly from the sale of wool from its Lakeland sheep farms. The Cistercian interest in agricultural and architectural improvement benefitted many local farms and villages. Biggar, Roose, Cocken, Hawcoat and Salthouse all came under Monastic patronage.

Furness Abbey, The Nave

I feel quite an old man now.

RELIABLE WR 63 SERIES.

...safe. What do you think of them?

85. A 1905 postcard of the Nave at Furness Abbey. A local legend relates how Sir Thomas Cromwell's troops sacked the Abbey after being made aware of its situation by the ringing of bells. The truth was more mundane. Only a handful of old or sick monks were left to 'surrender' to the troops. Lead was taken from the roof but most of the ruin was the result of harsh weather on soft sandstone and the use of the Abbey as a quarry by local inhabitants. Dalton Castle and Ulverston Church were both rebuilt with Abbey stone and old farms such as Sandscale and Peasholmes contain the odd monastic block.

BUCCLEUGH BRIDGE, BUCCLEUGH DOCK, BARROW IN FURNESS.

86. The Buccleuch Bridge reflected in the calm of Buccleuch Dock. This cantilever Bridge was built soon after the construction of Ramsden Dock and was used to carry a railway line to Barrow Island station, at a time when many Vickers workers caught the train to work. It could be lifted to allow the passage of shipping, as large as, for example, the Russian cruiser 'Rurik'. The postcard was printed in Germany, but the mis-spelling of Buccleuch is a common mistake – as a glance at the street sign on the corner of Duke Street and Buccleuch Street will testify! The bridge was dismantled in 1971, removing a distinctive landmark in Barrow's dock scenery.

High Level Bridge, Barrow-in-Furness.

87. The High Level Bridge, forming part of Michaelson Road from the town centre to Barrow Island, photographed in the late 1920s. This structure was opened in 1886 and replaced an earlier swing bridge. It was financed partly by the Borough Council and partly by the Furness Railway, who at that time owned Barrow Island. The abutments on the Hindpool Road side were carved in limestone from Stainton Quarry and the centre panel bore the arms of John Fell, Mayor of Barrow at the time the work was commenced. A modern cantilever bridge replaced it in 1968 at a cost of over £800,000.

88. A panoramic view of Devonshire Dock and its surrounding industries. The Devonshire Dock was opened on 19 September 1867 by the Duke of Devonshire. At the evening banquet W.E. Gladstone visualised the port of Barrow as a possible rival to Liverpool. It was a heady time as a few months earlier Barrow had received its Charter of Incorporation as a Borough. The postcard shows the floating dock complete with merchant ship, railway workings and, in the background, the now abandoned Graving Dock. Barrow's dock system was completed with the building of Buccleuch Dock (1873), Ramsden Dock (1879) and Cavendish Dock (1880).

89. Work nears completion on the Naval Airship Shed on Cavendish Dock, a postcard published in 1909. By the time Cavendish Dock was finished it had become obvious that Barrow's growth was at an end and that the new dock was surplus to requirements. Various attempts were made to make it useful – including an outdoor floating baths (which sank in a gale!) – and the Airship Shed was ordered by the Admiralty in 1909. Airship No. 1 was built there and had a satisfactory first trial. In September 1911, however, the 'Mayfly' broke her back, due largely to inherent design faults predicted by Vickers' engineers. Successful airships at Barrow had to wait until after the Great War.

90. A 1900 promotional card of the Vickers Works on Barrow Island, complete with very full slipways. The first shipyard at Barrow was the Barrow Shipbuilding Company, formed in 1871 largely with Furness Railway capital. In 1888 the yard was bought by the Naval Construction Company and the specialisation in Admiralty orders began. Vickers took over in 1897 and were able to combine shipbuilding with heavy engineering. They benefitted directly from the expansion of World navies at the beginning of this century, winning contracts from Russia, Japan, Brazil, China, Peru, Chile and Turkey. With the decline of the Furness Railway and the Steelworks, the arrival of Vickers had given Barrow's economy some hope for the future.

160 TON CRANE LIFTING "HOLLAND" CLASS SUBMARINE.

91. One of the 'Holland' submarines in transit at Vickers Works, probably in 1902. In 1900 the Admiralty somewhat reluctantly ordered five submarines of the 'Holland design', each 63 feet long with a submerged displacement of 120 tons. Vickers launched No. 1 on 2 October, 1901, and it was completed the following year, as were the other four vessels. Their speed was eight knots at surface, five knots submerged and they had a crew of seven. Whilst they proved trail-blazers for submarines in the Royal Navy, their service records were less than glorious — No. 1 sold for scrap 1913, No. 2 sold in 1913, No. 3 sunk in 1911, No. 4 dismantled in 1912, No. 5 sank in tow for the breakers.

H.M. SUBMARINE A1.

S CRIBB

92. Submarine 'A1' in smooth waters, photographed some time between 1902 and 1904. Originally laid down as the sixth 'Holland', the 'A1' was adapted into a one hundred feet submarine, with a speed of eleven knots at surface, seven knots submerged. It was launched by Vickers on 9 July 1902 but in 1904, during fleet manouvres near Spithead, the 'SS Berwick Castle' collided with the 'A1'. Eleven submariners were killed in Britain's first underwater tragedy. It was later raised and sold in 1911. A further twelve more A Class submarines were built from 1903 to 1905; most were sold for scrap in 1919 or 1920.

93. The four-masted barque 'Euterpe' tied up at Barrow Docks, probably in the 1890s. She was built by the Barrow Shipbuilding Company for Wenke and Sons of Hamburg and was launched on 15 March 1884. The 'Euterpe' was 282 feet long and had a displacement weight of 3,000 tons. About the same time two other four-masted barques were built for the Earl Line (David Brown and Sons) – the 'Earl of Jersey' and the 'Earl of Chatham'. A few years later two three-masted oil tankers (the 'Hainaut' and the 'Unionen') were built by the Naval Construction Company. In September 1902 the 'Euterpe' blew up and sank off the Scillies on her way to Chile with a cargo of coal. Seven lives were lost.

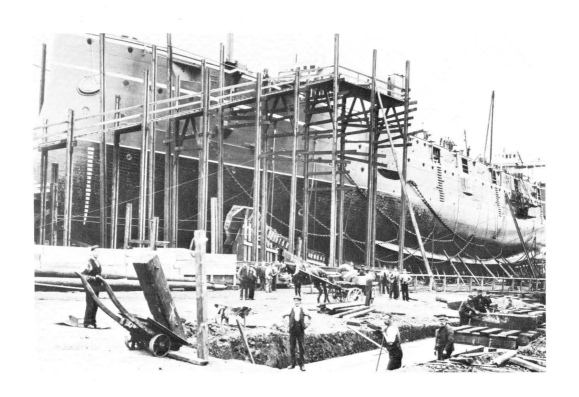

94. A temporary lull at the Shipyard during the construction of the 'Amphitrite', some time in 1897. The 'Amphitrite' was a 'Diadem' Class Cruiser almost identical to the 'Niobe'. She had a displacement of 11,000 tons, cost about £600,000 and had a crew of 670 officers and men. She was launched in January 1898 and completed in 1900. From 1902 to 1905 the 'Amphitrite' served on the China Station and was then in the Chatham and Devonport Reserves. For a few months during the Great War she joined the Atlantic North Cruiser Squadron, but was then put in the Portsmouth Reserve and later converted into a minelayer. She was scrapped at Milford Haven in 1920.

95. Two warships fitting out beneath the 150 feet crane in Devonshire Dock. Nearest the side is the 'HMS Triumph', originally ordered by the Chilean government and launched as the 'Libertad' in March 1902. She was purchased in December 1903 by the Royal Navy for £937,500 and completed in June 1904. On 25 May 1915 she was torpedoed by 'U21' off the Dardanelles. Alongside her in the photograph is 'HMS Dominion', launched in August 1903 and completed in July 1905. From 1914 to 1917 she served in the Third Battle Squadron and then became a depot ship. She was sold for scrap to Thos. Ward Ltd. and was broken up at Preston in 1924.

96. The spick-and-span Furness Railway tug, 'Cartmel', photographed soon after its launch in August 1907. It is a mistake to imagine that the Barrow shipyard built only pioneering submarines, mighty warships or noble liners. These may have been the stars, but the also-rans were needed to keep the yard busy — tugs, floating docks, colliers, barges, a lifeboat. In the desperate years after the Great War, Vickers were glad enough to win any contract, no matter how modest. The 'Cartmel' was a rare example of the use of local names. Only one vessel was called the 'Barrow' — an inglorious sludge vessel built in 1892 for London County Council.

97. Perhaps the most tragic ship to be built by Vickers, the battleship 'Vanguard', launched on 22 February 1909. Built at a time of 'big ship madness', she had a displacement of 19,250 tons and her main armaments were ten twelve inch guns. During the Great War she joined the First Battle Squadron and saw action at the Battle of Jutland in 1916. The following year, on 9 July, she was sunk whilst at anchor in Scapa Flow. An internal explosion ripped her apart and there were only two survivors from her complement of 850 officers and men. 'Vanguard' was recovered during the salvage operations in which ships of the scuttled German Fleet were raised.

98. A 1913 postcard of the Brazilian warship 'Sao Paulo' leaving Barrow in July 1910. Completed at a cost of £1,800,000 the 'Sao Paulo' had a displacement of 19,281 tons, and was armed with twelve 12 inch guns plus thirty smaller guns. She was crewed by 900 officers and men. Little seems to have happened to 'Sao Paulo' during her career. For five years after 1946 she lay idle at Rio de Janeiro and was then sold to an English yard for scrap. On 20 september 1951 she was towed away by the tugs 'Bustler' and 'Dexterous', but about 150 miles off the Azores contact with her was lost and the 'Sao Paulo' was never seen again.

99. A spectacular side launch of the 'Solimoes' in Walney Channel, 9 August 1913. Built for the Brazilian government as a River Monitor, and sister ship to the 'Javary' and 'Madeira', she was taken over by the Admiralty for service in the Great War and renamed 'HMS Severn'. On 11 July 1915, together with 'HMS Mersey' (formerley the 'Madeira'), she sank the German Cruiser 'Koenigsberg' in the Rufiji River off East Africa. This engagement was the first time that naval fire was directed by aerial intelligence. The 'Severn' was sold for scrap in 1921.

100. The launch of one of Barrow's most famous ships, the 'Jervis Bay', 17 January 1922. A sister ship to the 'Moreton Bay' and 'Hobson's Bay', she was built for the Australian Commonwealth Government Line. In 1928 she was bought by Lord Kylsant and five years later by the Aberdeen and Commonwealth Line. During the War she was converted into an Armed Merchant Cruiser and deployed as a convoy escort. On 5 November 1940, to the south of Iceland, she came upon the German battleship 'Admiral Scheer'. By gallantly engaging the 'Scheer', the 'Jervis Bay' allowed over thirty convoy ships to escape. The 'Jervis Bay' was sunk and her captain awarded the Victoria Cross.

LAUNCH OF H. M. S. CUMBERLAND, AT BARROW. MARCH 16TH.1926.

101. An action shot of the 'Cumberland', a 'Kent' class cruiser launched in 1926. This was the first warship built by Vickers after the industrial depression which immediately followed the Great War. She had a displacement of 9,750 tons, a maximum speed of just over thirty-one knots, and was one of the 'Cherry Tree' vessels whose size had been cut down by the terms of the Washington Naval Treaty. The 'Cumberland' served on the China Station and then during the Second World War saw action in the South Atlantic, the Home Fleet, the Eastern Fleet and the East Indies. After a period as a trials vessel she was sold for scrap, visiting Barrow for a farewell call in October 1958.

102. A peaceful enough setting for what was to become a historic vessel. The 'Kedah' was built for the Straits Steamship Company of Singapore to serve as a feeder ship for the Blue Funnel Line. She was launched in July 1927 and completed four months later. After a chequered career she was bought in 1946 by the Kedem Israel Line, registered at Haifa and renamed 'Kedmah' ('Eastward'). She carried 260 passengers and was the first ship to raise the flag of the new state of Israel. A second change of name followed in 1952 when she was sold to Harris and Dixon and called 'Golden Isles'. Four years later she was scrapped at Newport.

103. A tight squeeze for the 'Orontes' as she leaves Barrow in July 1929. She was built for the Orient line, was over six hundred feet long, could accommodate sixteen hundred passengers and had a crew of over six hundred. During the War she served as a troopship and escaped several submarine attacks. She re-entered private service in 1948 and was worked until 1962. On the 5 March of that year she arrived at Valencia to be broken for scrap by the Italian firm of Ordaz and Company. Other Orient liners built by Vickers included the 'Orama', 'Otranto' and 'Orford' – the latter was sunk off Toulon in May 1940 when being used as a troop carrier.

7744   DUKE STREET, BARROW-IN-FURNESS.   SANKEYS

104. A busy town centre scene, probably in the early 1920s. The taxi rank outside the Town Hall was a well-known feature of Barrow life and lasted until the present Civic Hall was built in the late 1960s. Horse cabs had waited there from the 1870s — an irate cabman wrote to the old 'Barrow Herald' asking the Council to build a shelter. A neat little building was later erected, only to be described as a public convenience by an urban historian on a flying visit to Barrow. The statue is of Frederick Cavendish, assassinated by Irish nationalists at Dublin in 1882. It now stands at the junction of North Road and Hindpool Road.

7745   DUKE STREET, BARROW-IN-FURNESS.   SANKEYS.

105. Halfway along Duke Street, at the junction with Cavendish Street and St. Vincent Street, photographed in the mid-1920s. Ashurst's, the fruiter and florist shop, is now occupied by the rebuilt Cumbria County Council careers office. C.T. Studholme is described in a 1924 Directory as a mantle warehouseman, by which was meant ladies and gentlemen's outfitters. These are now a building society premises. A few yards further along is a parked vehicle, almost certainly the earliest motorised carrier used by Robinson and Son, Auctioneers. Sixty years later there is still transport of goods in and out of the showrooms, only the removal van has changed.

Tram Terminus & Town Hall, Barrow in Furness.

106. A crowd obligingly poses for the photographer in Schneider Square. Although the card was sent in 1924 the photo must have been taken a year or two before, since by then the plumbing business of Hayman Blumenthal (advertised on the tram) had ceased, after more than forty years in Cavendish Street. The statute commemorates Henry William Schneider, mineowner and co-founder of the Iron-works, colleague and rival of Ramsden in both business and politics. Where Ramsden was stolid and discreet, Schneider was inventive and controversial. Schneider bitterly resented Ramsden's knight-hood, his own lack of recognition probably being the price of being found guilty of corruption at the Lancaster Parliamentary election of 1865.

107. A morning tram near Salthouse Railway Bridge in 1924. The Town Hall to Roose route was one of the original tracks opened in 1885. A Furness Railway tourist guide in 1886 was less than flattering about the trip: 'The tram passes St. George's Church, the Vulcan steel works and St. Luke's Church, then on to the wilds of Roose where there is nothing to attract the traveller but the return tram.' At least from August 1923 a connecting bus service allowed escape to Rampside and two years later it was extended along the new Coast Road. Trams continued at Barrow until 5 April 1932, when the last one was driven in by William Parsons — the driver of the first ever steam tram in July 1885!

108. Street games in North Row, Roose, in the late 1920s. Whilst the settlement of 'Rosse' was mentioned in the Domesday Book, the cottages of North and South Row date back to the 1870s when they were built by the Steelworks to house miners at the newly discovered Stank iron mines. The vast majority of the original settlers were Cornish miners and this accounts for the village church being named after the Cornish Saint Perran. Roose remained a mining village until the Stank mines were closed in 1901, since when it has slowly lost its separate identity. Almost gone as well are the distinctive Hawcoat sandstone fronts and the lobby shared by two cottages.

YACHTING AT PIEL ISLAND. 204. J. ATHERTON BARROW

109. Yachts racing in the channel with Piel Island in the background, a 1925 postcard. Piel has been used as a safe harbour from monastic times and possibly earlier. The Castle was in fact built as a fortified warehouse for the storage of Furness Abbey wool awaiting shipment to continental markets. A public house is still kept on the island, the landlord being traditionally crowned 'King of Piel'. Yachting regattas were held off Roa in the 1870s and 1880s, the climax being a race from Liverpool to Piel for the Ramsden trophy. It is still a popular boating centre, as any visit on a summer weekend will testify.

RAMPSIDE.

110. A 1907 postcard of Rampside by W. Cookson, photographer, of Dalton Road, Barrow. At the beginning of the last century Rampside was a popular holiday resort, an equal of the cross-bay Poulton-le-Sands (later called Morecambe). William Wordsworth spent a holiday at Rampside and frequently visited Furness Abbey. To accommodate visitors James Clarke opened the 'New Inn' in 1840, later renamed the 'Clarke's Arms'. In 1800, when Rampside had a population of 94, the nearby hamlet of Barrow could only muster 64. Such was the growth of the new town, however, that in 1881 Rampside became the last major addition to the territory of the Borough of Barrow-in-Furness.

111. A country scene at the home of the Wadham family, Millwood near Furness Abbey. The mansion belonged to the Duke of Buccleuch, for whom Edward Wadham served as mineral agent from about 1856. He was one of the town's first Councillors in 1867, Mayor from 1878 to 1881 and when he died in 1913 he was succeeded by his son Walter. Millwood had a staff of thirteen before the Great War and even had a small branch line off the Railway for the transport of goods. When Walter Wadham died in 1945 Millwood was closed and two years later it was sold to Lancashire County Council for use as an old people's home.

112. A close-up view of High Cocken, perched on the edge of Hawcoat Quarry. This modest cottage was the home of George Romney, artist, from 1742 to 1755. Born at Beckside in Dalton and educated for a time at Dendron Church school, Romney went on to become one of the most celebrated of English eighteenth century artists. He also briefly owned Low Cocken, a farmstead which was eventually bought by Barrow Steelworks and whose land was used to accommodate the tipping of waste slag. Hawcoat Quarry supplied much of the stone for Barrow's public buildings, including the extensive dock system. Two rows of houses — Chester and Bradford Streets — were built to house quarrymen.

113. A stiff westerly stretches the flag at the Tea House above Romney's Cottage. One of the Furness Railway's ideas to attract tourist traffic was to convert Romney's Cottage into a Museum and incorporate it into a regular tour programme. The most common trip included a visit to Furness Abbey and then a coach ride to the Romney Museum, followed by a journey to Walney Island. From the hill top Tea House the views of the Lake District to the north and east would have been superb – but to the south and west lay the Ironworks, Slagbank and what was then a smokey Barrow-in-Furness. As with the 'Lady Evelyn' voyages, the Romney tours were never resumed after the Great War.

114. A classic study of leafy suburbia, photographed about 1915. The original Crosslands House was built in the 1860s for J.T. Smith, manager of the Iron and Steelworks and it remained a private residence until 1925 when it was converted into Our Lady's Convent. When some of the estate lands were sold for development in the last years of the nineteenth century the name was subtly and inexplicably abbreviated. On the left are numbers 59-61 (with large balcony) and numbers 63-65 (the small balconies have now been removed). Present day trees block out the house on the right and the view to open fields at the rear.

Love to all at Home.

THE PARK.

115. The last two postcards are something of a mystery. They were not sent through the post so we can offer no definite date. Is one of the women Gladys Cooper, the famous British actress? Were they cards sent to the Front during the Great War? They were certainly mass produced and must have their equivalent in many towns. The scenes depicted in the series were of the Barrow Park, the James Dunn Park, Furness Abbey, and the residential end of Abbey Road. Forty or fifty years previously Barrow's pride in its economic growth would have demanded pictures of the Ironworks, the Railway, the docks and a town mansion built on the profits of heavy industry.

With love to a dear Friend.

116. Whatever their exact date of publication was, these postcards are symbolic of a time when keeping in touch meant writing a card rather than using the telephone. Our selection includes holiday messages of the traditional 'having a grand time, wish you were here' type. But many contain little more than trivial domestic and travel information. The Rampside card (number 110) was posted off to relations at Biggar Village, which could easily be seen across the channel! The locally produced card is now a thing of the past; a 21st Century 'Barrow-in-Furness in old picture postcards' will never be published – unless there is a video version!

Duke St.

Cavendish Square

High Level Bridge

BARROW-IN-FURNESS

Abbey Rd.

Ramsden. Square